A Children's Book About

DISOBEYING

Managing Editor: Ellen Klarberg
Copy Editor: Annette Gooch
Editorial Assistant: Lana Eberhard
Art Director: Jennifer Wiezel
Production Artist: Gail Miller
Illustration Designer: Bartholomew
Inking Artist: Berenice Happé Iriks
Coloring Artist: Berenice Happé Iriks
Lettering Artist: Linda Hanney
Typographer: Communication Graphics

A Children's Book About

DISOBEYING

By Joy Berry

GROLIER ENTERPRISES CORP.

This book is about Annie.

Reading about Annie can help you understand and deal with **disobeying.**

You are disobeying when you do not do what you have been told to do.

Your parents have good reasons for telling you what to do. This is why you should not disobey them.

Your parents tell you what to do because they do not want you to hurt yourself or others.

Your parents tell you what to do because they do not want you to damage or destroy things.

Your parents tell you what to do because they want you to be liked by other people.

Your parents tell you what to do because they want you to be fair.

Sometimes you might wonder why parents get to tell their children what to do.

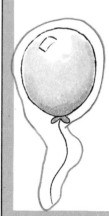

Parents tell their children what to do because they have lived longer and have learned more than children.

Thus, parents usually know what is best for their children.

Parents tell their children what to do because they are responsible for their children.

Parents have to take care of the damage when their children hurt themselves or others.

Sometimes parents need to punish their children for disobeying.

The purpose of a punishment is to make children feel bad about disobeying so they will not disobey again.

You can avoid being punished if you do these things:

- Talk to your parents.
- Find out what they want you to do. Then do it.

Sometimes you might not agree with your parents. Tell them how you feel.

They might change their minds. If they do not change their minds, drop the subject.

Nagging and throwing tantrums will only frustrate you and make your parents angry.

CAN'T I EAT SOME CANDY BEFORE DINNER, IF I EAT ONLY A LITTLE BIT?
NO! EVEN A LITTLE BIT OF CANDY WILL TAKE AWAY YOUR APPETITE FOR DINNER.
MAYBE I SHOULD HOLD IT UNTIL AFTER DINNER.

Tell the truth if you disobey.

Admit that you disobeyed.

Say that you are sorry and mean it.

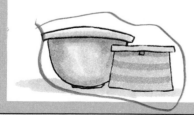

Accept your punishment if you disobey.

Do not be angry at your parents when they punish you. Remember, it was you who disobeyed, not them.

Try not to disobey again.

When you obey, you please your parents, and you are doing what is best for you.